Amherst Sonrise Church of the Nazarene

MW01121220

Glenda Smithers

Beacon Hill Press of Kansas City
Kansas City, Missouri

Copyright 1998 by
Beacon Hill Press of Kansas City

Printed in the United States of America

ISBN 083-411-6839

Editor: Bruce Nuffer
Assistant Editor: Kathleen M. Johnson
Cover Design: Keith Alexander
Illustrations: Roland Miller

Unless otherwise indicated, all Scripture quotations are taken from the *Holy Bible, New International Version*® (NIV®). Copyright © 1973, 1978, 1984 by International Bible Society. Used by permission of Zondervan Publishing House. All rights reserved.

Note: This book is part of the *Understanding Christian Mission,* Children's Mission Education curriculum. It is designed for use in Year 3, Compassionate Ministries. This study year examines the importance of helping others.

10   9   8   7   6   5   4   3   2   1

To
Hazel and Irene
and all the real Mrs. Spainhowers

Contents

CHAPTER 1

A Dinner Guest

Jarina climbed the stairs. She opened the door to her house, using her key. Inside, newspapers lay across the carpet, over the sofa, and on top of the TV.

"Mama, I'm home from school," Jarina called.

A voice from the kitchen answered, "Don't throw away my newspapers. I want to keep looking for a job. I already started dinner. Take your bath and change into your playclothes."

Jarina sang as she splashed the warm bathwater over her body. She was excited. Tomorrow morning she would help Mrs. Spainhower plan a special dinner. Mrs.

Spainhower was a city mission worker at the Main Street Shelter.

Jarina bathed, then dressed and went to the kitchen.

"Meat loaf! Tonight? Are we having company?" Jarina asked when she stepped into the kitchen.

Mama nodded. "I asked Mrs. Spainhower to have dinner with us," she said. Mama placed the dish on their small kitchen table.

"Meat loaf is my favorite!" Jarina exclaimed.

"You'll eat anything," her mama teased.

"Why did you ask Mrs. Spainhower to dinner?" asked Jarina.

"She has been a good friend to us," Mama said. "She helps us and other families in our apartment complex. She drives me to the food pantry when the car won't run."

Later, Mrs. Spainhower arrived. She said a prayer for the food. As they ate, Jarina chatted about tomorrow's meeting.

"I hope lots of helpers show up at the mission," Mrs. Spainhower said. "We will need people to make invitations, hang decorations, and plan games."

"I've made up a poem for the party invitation!" Jarina said.

CHAPTER 2

Broken Wishbone

It was nine o'clock the next morning when Mrs. Spainhower came to pick up Jarina. Jarina's mama had a job interview at the doughnut shop, but her car wouldn't start.

"I will take you," said Mrs. Spainhower.

When they dropped off her mama, Jarina said, "I hope they hire you, Mama."

"Call me at the mission," said Mrs. Spainhower. "I will come get you when your interview is over."

"Thank you, Hazel." Mama's voice was soft. "You two have fun planning the dinner at the shelter."

When the traffic cleared, Mrs. Spainhower pulled away from the doughnut shop.

"I didn't know you could write such good poems!" she declared. "Will you tell me your poem again?"

> *Here's a little secret*
> *I will tell to you.*
> *A horn of plenty party!*
> *Come join us, please do!*

recited Jarina.

"Wonderful!" praised Mrs. Spainhower. When she and Jarina got to the shelter, there were girls and boys standing in groups on the sidewalk. All were laughing and talking.

"Come on, Jarina," Mrs. Spainhower said. "We have much to do before your mother calls. Will you help me carry sacks of supplies inside?"

Jarina nodded. She waved to the other children. She smiled when she saw DeShawn, a boy from her class at school.

As they went inside the building, a girl smiled at Jarina. "Hi!" she said. Her voice was shaky as she added, "I am Trubie. I live in the same apartments you do."

"Good, you can help me make invitations! I am Jarina Madison."

Trubie smiled. "My mama, papa, and twin baby brothers moved in last winter."

Right away, Jarina liked Trubie. Jarina thought she would be lots of fun.

Mrs. Spainhower sorted out supplies on a table. Jarina copied her poem on colored paper. Trubie drew a picture. The invitations said:

> Here's a Little Secret
> I Will Tell to You.
> A Horn of Plenty Party!
> Come Join Us, Please Do!
> November 26
> Main Street Shelter
> Party 4 o'clock
> Dinner 5 o'clock

Paper decorations began to fill the room. Some were filled with raisins and nuts to put on the tables. Others hung from the lights.

Somewhere down the hall a telephone rang. Mrs. Spainhower went to answer it.

Minutes later she returned and called Jarina's name.

"Jarina," repeated Mrs. Spainhower as she held her gently, "a hospital doctor called. Your mama has been in an accident. You wait in the car while I get my coat."

Trubie squeezed Jarina's hand.

DeShawn dug in his pocket and gave Jarina a real turkey wishbone. "Make a wish, then break it," he told her.

CHAPTER 3

Hillside Hospital

Leaving the shelter, Mrs. Spainhower and Jarina drove to a large building. Jarina could see it was an old building.

The two walked to the hospital door in silence. Inside, Mrs. Spainhower said, "I want to speak to your mama's doctor. Will you wait for me in the visitors' room?"

Jarina nodded her head without looking at her friend.

Mrs. Spainhower squeezed Jarina's hand as they walked into the hospital waiting room. The mission worker showed her where to sit, then went to see the doctor. Jarina looked out a big, glass window.

"I wish I were home. I wish I were climbing the stairs. I'd climb to my apartment. To my mama," thought Jarina.

On the sofa Jarina curled her legs up under her. She thought about her poem. She thought about Trubie and DeShawn. She could not understand why this happened to Mama.

Suddenly Jarina remembered DeShawn's wishbone. She pulled it from her sweater pocket. Was it good luck or bad luck to pull apart a wishbone? She forgot which it was, so she put it back inside her pocket.

Jarina thought about being a nurse someday. She looked forward to helping people.

Suddenly that thought made her cry. She couldn't even help her own mama. Where was Mama? Was she going to be OK? Why did God let this happen to Mama?

Mrs. Spainhower came back. She said to Jarina, "Your mama was hit by a car as she crossed Main Street. She's hurt, but the doctors will help her. You can see her now."

Mrs. Spainhower led Jarina down the hall and into an elevator.

They paused outside a door, then the mission worker knocked gently.

A voice called, "Come in." The doctor was just leaving Mama's room. He said hello to Jarina and reminded them not to stay long. "Mrs. Madison needs her rest," he told them.

Inside, Jarina saw her mama lying in a hospital bed. She wore a white hospital gown, printed with pink flowers. Her jet-black hair sat piled high on top of her head. Jarina thought she looked beautiful, even covered in bandages.

Mrs. Spainhower held one of Mama's hands, and so did Jarina. Mama's eyes were closed. There were wires going from Mama's body to a nearby TV-like machine. Jarina started to tremble.

Tears ran loose in her eyes. She took a deep breath, then she blurted it out. "Mrs. Spainhower, is my mama dead?"

Mama's eyelids fluttered. Then they blinked open. "Jarina?" she said, slowly moving her head. "I'm OK. Mrs. Spainhower is going to take care of you until I'm ready to go home."

CHAPTER 4

An Afternoon in the Park

After church Sunday, Jarina sat with Mrs. Spainhower on a park bench. They tossed seeds to the pigeons. A gray squirrel ran at the pigeons, sending them to the air.

"Did you see that bossy squirrel?" Mrs. Spainhower asked Jarina.

Jarina didn't hear her question. "I wonder if Mama is scared in the hospital," she said.

"If she is, she'll trust God," she replied. "Once she told me about the time you fell down the apartment stairway. Your arm broke in two places! She prayed a lot that day in the emergency room. She said that was a day she'll never forget."

"Why not?" asked Jarina.

The mission worker smiled. "Your mama accepted Christ as her Savior soon afterward."

"How did you know about us?" asked Jarina.

Mrs. Spainhower smiled. "I like getting to know the people in the community. The more I know about their needs, the more I can help."

The pigeons came back, and Jarina tossed more seeds. "I like to help! I gave my dollars to the Food for Famine Fund. Africa's crops did not grow. People did not have any food to eat."

Jarina paused. "Could we say a prayer for Mama, Mrs. Spainhower?"

"Sure," said Mrs. Spainhower. The two of them held hands and bowed their heads. On the park bench they asked God for a special blessing—a healthy body for Jarina's mama.

Suddenly, Mrs. Spainhower said, "I'm hungry. How about you?"

"I could eat anything!" exclaimed Jarina. "Let's go back to your house and eat!"

CHAPTER 5

Samson and Sandwiches

Inside the house, Jarina helped make chicken salad sandwiches. Mrs. Spainhower spread a blue-checkered tablecloth on the table. They took turns thanking God for the food.

Jarina took a big bite of the sandwich. She took a gulp of milk from her glass.

"Meow. Meow." A tiger-striped cat with marble eyes sat looking at Jarina from the top of a cabinet.

"I'm sorry, Samson," said Mrs. Spainhower. "That was rude of me not to introduce you to Jarina. Jarina, this is Samson. Samson, this is Jarina."

"Where did you find him?" asked Jarina.

"He was a stray begging for scraps at the shelter. One day I made the mistake of bringing him home."

Jarina looked at the fine-looking cat. "Mrs. Spainhower! You didn't make a mistake!" she said.

Jarina finished eating, then patted Samson. She wished her apartment complex allowed pets. The wish reminded her of Mama and home. She didn't want to cry in front of Mrs. Spainhower. So she looked around for something to talk about.

"Who are they?" asked Jarina, pointing to a framed picture.

Mrs. Spainhower told her that the couple were her parents. They were missionaries. "Missionaries in other lands do much the same work we do here."

Jarina nodded her head.

Mrs. Spainhower snapped her fingers as if she had an idea. "Would you like to put together a jigsaw puzzle with me in the parlor? It is a puzzle of Noah and the ark."

Jarina nodded again. That sounded like fun. The grandfather clock chimed two different times before the last piece was in place. The ark was filled with smiling animals.

Suddenly a real, live animal jumped on top of the round table. Puzzle pieces broke apart.

"SAMSON!" Mrs. Spainhower just shook her head. She shooed her cat away. "See, Jarina. It *was* a big mistake to bring home a stray!"

"That's OK, Mrs. Spainhower. It's the fun of working a puzzle that counts." She put the pieces back into the box.

Mrs. Spainhower put on her reading glasses. She sat in her rocker and rocked. She lifted her favorite book from an end table and placed it on her lap.

Jarina thought aloud. "I wonder what job God has for me when I grow up."

Her hostess peered over the rim of her glasses. "If I was to guess," she said to Jarina, "your job would be an exciting one with lots of responsibility."

Mrs. Spainhower went back to reading her Bible. Jarina smiled. She liked helping people. She wanted a job that would make her mama proud and something that God chose just for her.

The grandfather clock chimed again. Jarina went to the guest room. Her playclothes, pajamas, and underwear lay folded in drawers. Her good clothes already hung in the closet.

Jarina turned down the lavender quilt on the guest bed. She wasn't afraid to click off the light. Samson kept her company on the other pillow. She liked the happy purring he made.

As Jarina lay in bed, she talked to God.

Jarina was half asleep when she felt a kiss on her cheek. Not opening her eyes, she wondered if it was from Mrs. Spainhower or Samson.

CHAPTER 6

Old Enough for Mission

Jarina was busy at the shelter on Thursday.

First, she folded festive napkins for the long tables. Then she tied brown and yellow balloons in bunches.

Jarina looked around the Horn of Plenty room. She and Mama ate meals here when their money was low. When they had money, Mama always remembered to give something back. Jarina's clothes came from shelter thrift sales also. Jarina was thankful for the Main Street Shelter.

It was four o'clock. People came through the shelter doors. They laughed and talked. Turkeys warmed in the kitchen ovens. Lupe Lombardo carried in foil containers of food.

Bowls of thick gravy made with meat and spices looked so good!

Children filled the big room. Teenagers volunteered to care for the babies and toddlers.

Jarina sat on the floor. Inside she was both happy and sad. "Mama, I miss you," she thought again. After the food was put out, Mrs. Spainhower called the helpers into the kitchen. "Children," she said, "please watch for ways you can help. Run errands for mothers with their hands full. Carry plates for the older folks with walkers and canes. Help find lost coats when people go home. You are all wonderful helpers," she said. "Now go enjoy your special dinner!"

A pastor from the neighborhood prayed. He ended with a loud AMEN.

The meal was delicious. Jarina sat with Trubie's family. She watched Trubie's twin brothers eat so much she thought they might get sick!

Jarina and others helped clear the food away. "Where is Mrs. Spainhower?" Jarina asked another helper.

"Maybe in the nursery," said the older girl. "Why don't you pass the breadbaskets for a mission love offering?"

Jarina hurried to a shelf and counted out breadbaskets. She placed five breadbaskets around the room. If she were here, Mrs. Spainhower would also ask Jarina to put two empty boxes by the doors. "People," she had said, "like to give canned foods at holidays. If we don't give them the opportunity to give, we are taking a blessing away from them."

At the end of the evening Jarina thought she heard a quiet, whispering voice. It was a voice that she had heard before.

"It's your mama, Jarina!" Mrs. Spainhower called from the front doors. She held the door open wide for Mrs. Madison in her wheelchair.

Hands clapped for Jarina and her mother. Someone shouted a loud, "PRAISE THE LORD!"

Mama smiled and handed an empty plate to Jarina. "Am I too late for a turkey leg, honey?"

Jarina teased back. "All the food is gobbled down, Mama!"

"If it has been," said Mama, "*my* little girl ate most of it!"

"I will get you a hot meal from the kitchen," Mrs. Spainhower said.

Jarina hugged her mama. And she could not stop two or three happy tears.

"I am proud of you, Jarina. You have been a bright light for me and for Mrs. Spainhower. God is proud of you. I love you very much."

"Thank you," Jarina smiled. She would tell everybody how wonderful it was to be a helper for Jesus, a light for Christ in the world.